# ONLINE MONETIZATION

*7 Proven Ways to Make Passive Income Online*

A.T. Mezraim

## Copyright © 2018 (A.T. Mezraim)

All rights to this book are reserved. No permission is given for any part of this book to be reproduced, transmitted in any form or means; electronic or mechanical, stored in a retrieval system, photocopied, recorded, scanned, or otherwise. Any of these actions require the proper written permission of the publisher.

## Disclaimer

All erudition contained in this book is given for informational and educational purposes only. The author is not in any way accountable for any results or outcomes that emanate from using this material. Constructive attempts have been made to provide information that is both accurate and effective, but the author is not bound for the accuracy or use/misuse of this information.

# Contents

Introduction ..................................................................... 4

Freelancing ..................................................................... 7

Kindle eBooks ............................................................... 11

Affiliate Marketing ........................................................ 15

Online Advertisements ................................................. 21

Online Courses .............................................................. 26

Investing in Stocks ........................................................ 30

Royalties ........................................................................ 34

Recap ............................................................................. 38

A.T. Mezraim

# Introduction

*"How can I make money online?"*

*"What ways can I generate a passive income online without experience or a mind-boggling capital?"*

*"Can I make money from my YouTube Channel?"*

*"How can I monetize my blog?"*

These questions are being asked more frequently as time flies hard in this generation. People of all ages are interested in finding more use for their computers than gaming, watching movies, and generally doing things that do not bring it money.

There are two things you should know before proceeding. One will exhilarate you, but the other, not so much. The first is that you have the necessary instruments you need to engage successfully in this. You have a computer, a phone, internet connection, your willingness and interest, and this eBook.

However, the not so encouraging part is that making money online will not happen in a day. There is no button you will click to print money out. Neither is there any crossword puzzle you solve and get paid in millions. Rather, all routes you can take are long (but not necessarily complicated) ones which require utmost patience, steadfastness, and dedication before you can arrive at your destination of profit. One mistake made people who dally in this business but never do well is that they treat online income as a side thing. Meaning that they did not feel it is capable of exclusively providing for them and therefore do not put in enough work. In simple terms, they undermine its capabilities.

Engaging in online businesses means you are ready to treat it as the main thing, not just a thing. Also, if you do not have a YouTube Channel or any other means through which you can have a large audience, it is advisable to get one soon.

Compiled below are **seven** (proven) efficient methods through which one can generate a passive income online.

- Freelancing
- Kindle eBooks
- Affiliate Marketing

- Online Advertisements

- Online Courses

- Investing in Stocks

- Royalties

# Freelancing

A freelancer or a freelance worker is someone who is self-employed and decides not to work for a particular employer. Freelancers take on temporary contract jobs. They are sometimes represented by companies or temporary agencies which the freelancer has subscribed to. Freelancing is most prominent in music industries, writing, acting, computer programming, web design, translating, and illustrating and other forms of piece work.

Although freelancing is a little bit different from the other six methods, it is still one of the most preferred options. Some would argue and claim that freelancing is not very passive because, in freelancing, you trade your time and skill for money whereas passive incomes are supposed to be avenues where you can make money while sleeping.

However, using your skills happens to be one of the best ways to start out. It helps you to develop yourself as well as make money. Basically, you do exactly what you want and are paid for it.

What skills do you have? What can you do for people to pay you? That basically describes freelancing.

There are different methods through which freelancing can be done. We have freelancing surveys under which we have platforms such as Swagbucks. And we have freelancing marketplaces where you can sell your skills.

- **Swagbucks:** This website which is operated by Prodege LLC enables users to earn rewards by performing a variety of online activities including shopping, playing games, discovering online content and most importantly partaking in surveys. Swagbucks have a reward system whereby you can redeem points as retail gift cards and PayPal cash. Participating in a survey earns you up to about forty to two hundred Swagbucks. A hundred Swagbucks equals about one dollar. This method is quite fast and exciting, and not at all complicated. You can do this at your time and pace without any laid down hours.
- **Fiverr:** Fiverr is the world's largest marketplace for freelance services which are rendered at an affordable cost of five dollars per job performed. As at 2012, over

three million services were listed as available. This site is a great place where you can advertise your skills for a price. On this site, any and everything you are capable of doing can fetch you money. There are numerous amounts of skills that you can list on Fiverr. Basically, everything and anything can be monetized. People are willing to design book covers, make covers of songs, write, advertise, and basically anything for only 5 dollars. The name is probably derived from the basic amount of their gigs; five dollars - Fiverr. Not only is it a great place to find jobs, but it is also a great place to hire people.

- **Upwork:** Formerly known as Elance-oDesk, this site is similar to Fiverr and offers a wide range of services such as graphic designers, virtual assistants, and the likes. The main difference would be the lack of a fixed price which we have with Fiverr. Upwork has over twelve million registered freelancers, and five million clients. People from all over the world come here to advertise and hire services. It is a remarkable site to get things done quickly. It is also great for giving you a vast number and type of clientele since people from all over the world buy and sell services there.

If you are considering going into freelancing, keep in mind that it does not stop you from engaging in any of the other six methods which we will soon discuss. Also keep in mind that with freelancing, you set your own hours. This means that if you are not determined or self-disciplined to work, it would be quite disastrous for you financially because there is no one to dictate your hours.

There are also specific sites for specific freelancing jobs. For example, if your talent has to do with making and editing videos, there are special sites with jobs for freelance videographers. Similarly, there are special sites with jobs for freelance writers.

# Kindle eBooks

Kindle Store is an online eBook e-commerce store operated by Amazon as part of its retail website. It can be accessed from any Amazon Kindle, Fire tablet, or Kindle mobile app. At its launch in November 2007, the store had more than eighty-eight thousand (88,000) digital titles available. This number has increased by staggering amounts. As of December 2017, there were nearly 5.9 million available titles. Content on the store can be purchased online and downloaded through the easy and fast one-click purchasing.

Kindle Store is a great place to get eBooks on a broad collection of topics. On Kindle, you can find material about almost anything. It is also a very great place to make money. Users can also upload their written books to be bought. One great thing about Kindle is that books which were written ages ago can still generate income for their authors today. Put in the effort and write a book on a topic you know everyone wants to hear about, needs to hear about, or both. Choosing a topic of relevance is obviously important. It should be either about something people are searching for or something to pique interest. Before you even start writing, you have to research for material.

However, if you feel you do not have the skills to write a book but feel you have a great topic and a lot of research material, you can hire writers on any of the websites as mentioned earlier for freelancing. For about 80 cents, or 60 cents for 100 words you can get a writer. It, however, depends on what quality you want. Experienced writers may be priced higher. People who have had a lot of success on kindle go ahead even to publish their books in hardback. The better your content gets, the higher reviews you are given, hereby making your eBook more popular. Little wonder the income never stops.

You can also hire a freelancer to design a cover for your book. You may very well be able to do this yourself, but hiring is better because now you are a marketer and your time is precious. By hiring people, you are also gaining connections you will need as you grow more popular.

You can write a tutorial on any topic or basically anything. As I said, you may also source for research material and hire someone else to do your writing. It is advisable to write between 6000- 10,000 words. Remember that you can also hire another person to design a cover for you.

Researching the material is something you can skip provided you are ready to pay for it, of course. The material is available from freelancers on Epicrights. For a fee, you can get your research done for you.

Basically, you only need to have the will and money to invest. It is not too hard, and we have people who have built up ten thousand dollars a month passive income business just from this. Become a marketer and not a writer. Your time is the most valuable thing, so be willing to pay a little bit for people to do the work for you and then you become the marketing agent.

There is no specific amount of money you can be assured to earn. People have earned up to a thousand dollars weekly, and people have made less than one-tenth of that. An author who has a book with a five-star rating (and subsequently a lot of income) can have another book which generated a next-to-nothing income simply because of the weak content.

The great thing is that if you have just a book with great content and high ratings, you can use it to market yourself, market your skills, market other books you have written and even market other products. When people come across one good book you have written, they are eager to see more. Gradually, they start spending even more money on you.

# Affiliate Marketing

Affiliate marketing is a type of performance-based marketing in which a business rewards one or more affiliates for each visitor customer brought by the affiliate's own marketing strategies and efforts. Affiliate marketing outshines internet marketing to an extent because affiliates often use regular advertising methods such as organic search optimization (SEO), paid search engine marketing (PPC- Pay Per Click), e-mail marketing, content marketing, and to some extent display advertising.

Affiliate marketing is a well-known income generator. The fact that it displays passiveness at its best is also a plus. It is simply getting a commission for selling other people's products. This is great if you have a blog, website, or any other medium through which you can address people. The producers will give you a customized link and every time a purchase is made through you, you get a commission. It sounds just as easy as it really is.

Even if you do not have a blog or website, whatever way through which you can broadcast links is also alright. You can be given up to 50% commission depending on the product and producer and the popularity of whatever medium you use to broadcast the link. It is a great way to recommend products you use and enjoy to other people. By using this method, you are helping yourself, the producers and the buyers.

If you engage in affiliate marketing properly, you can base your whole market strategy on it and subsequently realize a staggering income.

Popular examples of people who engage in affiliate marketing are Oprah Winfrey, Casey Nesfat and a whole lot of famous people who advertise products. Oprah gets a cut from the sales of all those books which she recommends in her book club. She also gets a cut from the sales of all the items on "Oprah's Favorite Things." She is a great example of an affiliate marketer. Casey Netstat who is popular for making videos is also an affiliate marketer. For every buy on any item he lists such as his camera gear, he gets a cut. The amount on a single commission may not be huge, but when it adds up over time, it is worthwhile.

You are also allowed to use your creative thinking in any way that can attract people. This method of generating income is incredibly passive. You can have that dream of making money while you sleep. However, to earn such a useful amount of money, chances are you will have to advertise more than one product and through more than one avenue. This 'cost per click' method can bring in a sizable amount of income if you do it right.

Admittedly, this method is easier for those who have blogs or websites and similar media, because affiliates use their own websites, blogs, PPC campaigns, RSS and email to promote the products. Although, you can also use a YouTube Channel and any other media through which you can communicate with the public. Advertising a product is also a great way to increase to increase traffic on your site or blog spot (Blogging also happens to be an income generating method, although much less passive like freelancing) depending on how good the product in question is.

The next and logical question to ask would be how you can get these affiliate products to market or advertise. There are a number of sites which have options you would like; however, we will be looking at a few four.

1. **Clickbank:** Clickbank is a privately held internet retailer of both physical and digital products. This company has more than six million clients worldwide which makes it the 87th largest internet retailer. Clickbank is also an affiliate marketplace which makes it a great place to start. On Clickbank, there are a whole lot of products, services, and whatnots for you to pick from. Visiting this site gives you a wide range of choice.

2. **Affiliate.placed:** Another great option would be Affiliate.placed. Similar to Clickbank, products are available for marketing and advertisement. You can monetize your app even when users are not on it.

3. **ShareASale:** Based in the River North area of Chicago, ShareASale is also a trendy place to start. ShareASale services two customer sets in affiliate marketing: the affiliate and the merchant. On ShareASale, you also have a lot of products to choose from here. It has been in business for over seventeen years and has been strictly concerned with affiliate

marketing. Affiliates use ShareASale to identify promotable products to while earning a commission for referrals on those products. Affiliates use their own websites, blogs, PPC campaigns, RSS and email to promote the products. Merchants also use ShareASale to manage their affiliate program.

4. **Rakutenmarketing:** Rakuten is an affiliate marketing service provider. The company claims to be the largest pay-for-performance affiliate marketing available on the internet. Rakutenmarketing, like the others, gives you products which you can advertise. It was voted the number one affiliate marketing network for seven consecutive years.

All four sites are wonderful choices. You may use all four and market as many products as you would like. These options scream passive.

Of course, you do have to do some additional work which you will encounter such as creating the content and finding it and advertising it. Keep in mind that you cannot just market anything. You should market products which you would buy. Know your audience and satisfy them. That way, they will always listen to your recommendations. But remember that the lower the barrier is, the more flooded the place gets. The easier it is to make money off something, the less money you actually make from it. However, if you do a good job at affiliate marketing, it can work for you in ways it has not for others.

# Online Advertisements

Online advertising is a form of marketing to deliver promotional marketing messages to consumers.

You must not confuse affiliate marketing with advertisements. They are similar but quite different. Affiliate marketing basically has to do with links. However, advertisements are videos, short clips, pictures and things that are not just solitary links. Another vast difference is that with affiliate marketing, people have to actually buy before you can get paid off the commission. However, with an advertisement, just showcasing is enough. Once again, this choice would really suit people with blogs, YouTube Channels and similar methods of communication.

If you have a YouTube Chanel with a sizeable number of followers, displaying advertisements is a great way to generate income. Similarly, application programmers with free applications for download can insert these advertisements one way or another. People are known to make thousands of dollars from this alone.

Cost per mille (CPM) or cost per thousand (CPT) is a term regarding not only YouTube but also advertisements in general. It is an advertising term that simply means the cost an advertiser pays for a thousand views. CPM or CPT is calculated by dividing the cost of an advertising placement by the number of impressions which will be expressed in thousands which are generated. CPM or CPT is a must know term because it helps to calculate the relative efficiency of various advertising opportunities which simply means it finds out if advertising through a certain medium is worthwhile.

From a video with less than half a million views, three to five thousand dollars can be earned. So, if you see a video with a million views, the channel probably made above five thousand dollars off that video Affiliate marketing, and advertising can be combined into one to give you an even higher income. If you have a blog, YouTube channel or anything similar, this is a very great idea. Although blog advertisements are ubiquitous, there is nothing to say you cannot also do it. But remember that since others are doing it, you have to find your own uniqueness to make profits.

You must know your audience. Knowing them will help you know what to advertise. Although, it is obvious that you cannot know them individually, start with their age range. From there, you have a clue on who they are and subsequently, what to advertise. It is quite wrong to have a blog spot on sports and not have a single advertisement relating to sports. There is no substitute for knowing your audience.

Combining affiliate marketing and advertising is a very wise idea. There is no limit to the number of passive income generators you may engage in simultaneously.

Some other methods under advertisements are *brand deals* and *sponsorship*. These methods involve the use of YouTube accounts.

- Brand Deals: With the rapid increase of subscribers to YouTube, producers are eager to get channels through which they can be advertised. So basically, what happens is that you are paid to promote a brand. However, it is not a one-time thing. It involves drawing up of contacts for a long-time business relationship. Often, in YouTube videos, you see specific products placed in specific places with brand logos on them. Or you notice that reference is being made more often than not to a product. It simply tells that that channel has been engaged in a brand deal.

- Sponsorship: Similar to brand deals, a YouTube channel is paid to advertise a product. However, in this case, a sponsor takes over the costs of production of the video, and every other cost relating to the channel. It is basically the same as brand deals but with little differences.

Brand deals and sponsorships are different because you must have an audience. If you would like to know exactly how much your site is worth for sponsorship or brand deals, visiting Socialbluebook is the right thing to do. This site can tell you just how many subscribers you have, as well as what your average views per video are. It can also say what your engagement is how much minimum you should charge.

# Online Courses

Online courses are a great way to make money. They are also a great way to learn. Online courses on basically every topic are available. There are courses on how to start up a blog, how to open a YouTube account how to start up a YouTube channel, how to maintain a YouTube channel, how to make passive income with your business, how to manage your business, how to do basically anything and everything. There are also courses to help you be a master content researcher. There are even courses to answer more straightforward questions such as how do I get a brand logo? How do I come up with content that people will look for? How do I get my videos found? How do I adapt to the ever-changing algorithm? How do you monetize it? How can I monetize my blog? There are courses that not only answer any question you may have but put you through them in details.

There are online courses of different natures. That makes things much easier because you simply have to pick a useful topic which you know and teach people. One commonly used method to find interesting topics is to make online courses on problems which you have encountered yourself. It is a great idea because you will be speaking on a topic which you have firsthand knowledge of.

The hardest part of creating online courses is gathering enough knowledge on the said topic. Gathering knowledge is not a one-day thing. It is hardly ever even a one-week thing since knowledge is something you can never have fully. What you must do is present the knowledge which you do have in a way that will not only gain viewers' attention but in a way that will educate them. In simple terms, give them your knowledge without the stress it took you to gain it.

And, again, as the barrier to entry gets higher, the money you make gets higher as well. If it is hard to make money through something, the chances are that fewer people will be interested; thereby giving the few more opportunities to excel.

To improve your content, do not limit yourself to just creating with enthusiasm; instead, watch other online courses made by people you do not know. People have been in whatever field you chose before you. They are most likely more knowledgeable than you are. Watching online courses will be a big help to you. There will always be something to learn which you can add to your own course to make yourself better.

If you are wondering how to make an online course, a site called teachable would be a great place to start. This site not only helps you create online courses but also gives you a platform to sell. They can help you launch your course with minimal stress. At a monthly fee of around 39 dollars a month and a reasonable 5% transaction fee (Clickbank charges 7%) you can get all the help you need. Teachable is a great site, and it will help you if you can look into it. They also have free course bundle worth five hundred and sixty dollars ($560) to start you off. Using teachable, over a hundred million dollars ($100m) have been made by their twenty-two thousand (22k) instructors in sales of online courses. This gives us an average of five thousand dollars ($5k) per instructor. Teachable also has a professional plan and a basic plan so you can pick.

Udemy is another viral site that can help you too. With over twenty million students from around the world as subscribers and over seven hundred thousand courses, it is safe to say that Udemy is very useful. They offer courses on IT and software, programming languages, development, business, web development and many more. This site will also help you create your online course and allow you to sell to your audience. They are very helpful and reduce the stress of the whole process. Udemy has a cheaper offer; however, you do not own the content you upload when you subscribe to this offer and they can counter-fix any price they want. Udemy cuts prices you fix by as much as ninety percent. However, you can stop them from doing that by paying the full 40 dollars a month. Then, you own your content and can set the price without any interference.

# Investing in Stocks

The stock of a corporation consists of the all the owner's equity stock. A single share of the stock represents a fractional ownership of the corporation.

Before investing in stocks, always check with a professional. Often, we have heard *"Just go out and invest in stocks"* while this advice is enthusiastic, it is terrible. A sure way to lose money is by investing in stocks based on your own knowledge. Check with a professional and even then, use your head seeing as it is your own money. Investing in stocks is one of the most passive income generators. It also has a higher risk. Remember, the easier it gets, the more people flood in and the harder it gets, the fewer people you see.

If you are looking for a way to make passive income, chances are you do not have a lot of money to throw away you are looking for a way to earn money and not lose it. Investing in stocks which you have no or insufficient knowledge about is a dangerous thing to do. Therefore, before you invest, you must garner enough knowledge on your proposed investment. You should also try as much as possible to have the backing of a good brokerage firm. Charles Schwab is great discount brokerage firm. You can open an account there. They also pay a good interest of about 2 to 3 percent which is rare. If you want to trade, you can go through them and place trades in the market.

An important term when dealing with stocks is an *index fund*. An index fund, also known as index tracker is a mutual or exchange-traded fund designed to follow certain preset rules. These rules may include tracking prominent indexes or implementation rules such as tax management large block trading, tracking error minimization, patient or flexible trading strategies that allow for greater tracking error but lower market impact costs.

Index funds basically try to match the market average by owning a lot of it. Averagely, they grow between five to seven percent a year. In simple terms, you can make about two to five percent of your money year after year. That is passive income at its best. It will also be great to look into Lifecycle funds.

Remember, do your own research. Never take a stock recommendation so seriously that you do not do your own research. Investing money in stocks is an exciting thing to do. It is even more exciting when you make a profit. Do your research and do not be afraid to take risks. It is probably best to advise all beginners not to invest large amounts of money at first. Give yourself time to learn the about the stock market in general. Of course, the amount of money you make depends on what you invest. However, do not let that drive you into investing recklessly.

Individual funds are riskier than index funds. Because if the company you are investing in falls, all your investment in that company go down; you lose it all. That is the risk that comes with it. And that risk is perhaps what gives the thrill of investing. Remember, the more difficult the entry is, the fewer people that actually do enter.

A lot of people do nothing but invest in dividend stocks. That idea could suit you perfectly because once you get to a certain age, your priorities switch from trying to get as much money as possible to try and keep as much money as possible.

A payment made by a co-operation to its shareholders, usually as a distribution of profits is called a dividend. When a co-operation earns profits or surplus, the co-operation can re-invest the profit in business while they pay part of this profit to its shareholders as a dividend. Public companies usually pay dividends on fixed schedules but may declare a dividend at any time which is called a special dividend. Cooperatives deal differently. They allocate dividends based on members' activities, so their dividends are often considered as a pre-tax expense.

The lovely thing about stocks is that they take so little of your time that you still have enough time and energy to engage in other income generating tasks. That is a classic example of 'passive income.'

# Royalties

The last way on our list to make passive income online is through royalties. Royalties are what you get when you set up a created piece of art, music, video, application or other related things. Kindle eBooks are a good example of places that give royalties. They give you royalties for things you write.

Some other examples of applications which royalties are:

- **Spotify:** Spotify is a music, podcast, and video streaming service. It is a freemium service which means having the application is free but there are charges for additional services. Freemium is a medley of 'free' and 'premium.' Spotify's basic features are free with advertisements while other features such as improved streaming quality and downloads are offered via paid subscriptions. Artists who have their songs on Spotify get royalties each time their song is streamed. They also get money from their albums. The average Spotify stream costs between 0.006 cents and 0.008 cents. Admittedly, it is not much but if you multiply that by a million and you have a large amount of money. This means if your song is streamed on Spotify, you automatically make around six thousand dollars. Using Spotify is a great way to earn royalties. By our calculations, even if only a million people play your songs per month (that is around thirty-two thousand [32,000] streams per day), you have an income of five thousand dollars ($5,000) monthly. Basically, you create music and do nothing else while the royalties roll in.

- **Shutterstock:** Shutterstock is a well-known American provider of stock photography, stock footage, stock music and editing tools. Shutterstock has a library of about one hundred and twenty-five million (125 million) royalty-free stock photos, vector graphics, and illustrations. As well as over 4 million video clips and music clips available for licensing. This site has videos that were filmed by users and sold to Shutterstock. Shutterstock becomes the middleman and sells them to its active customer base of 1.4 million people in 150 countries. Shutterstock, when used properly can generate a substantial income. To get started, reach out to platforms such as this and ask about their policies on buying footage from artists, and buying footage from videographers. There are a lot of companies like that. All that is required is you filming it, getting the idea and reaching out to them. If you do it correctly, then that could be a way you can make income. Remember the higher the barrier, the lesser the population.

- **Envato** - ThemeForest: Envato is a mother site to a group of digital markets that cut across several digital fields with creative assets ranging from web design to themes, graphics, videos, web scripts, photography, audio and 3D models. With over 5 million items for sale, Envato till date has seen over 1.5 million active users (strictly buyers and sellers) as well as over 8 million members in the e-community. It is the highest trafficked marketplace. Under Envato, we have ThemeForest, CodeCanyon, VideoHive, AudioJungle, GraphicRiver, PhotoDune, and 3dOcean as marketplaces. Themeforest, according to Alexa is the 204th most visited site in the world. ThemeForest is an excellent repository of themes for WordPress as well as static websites. With the large amounts of people trooping into blogging, a decent income can be made from this. There are different background themes which different people have made which differ in price. On this marketplace, you can buy themes from fifty dollars ($50) all the way to one hundred and fifty ($150) dollars. So, if you are good at designing web pages from the scratch, or have coding experience, you can create themes and sell them here. You upload them there and royalties each time someone downloads them. You can also visit all the other branches(GraphicRiver, VideoHive, AudioJungle, CodeCanyon, PhotoDune, and 3dOcean) under Envanto as they have similar functions.

# Recap

Basically, you have gone through seven of the best ways to make passive incomes. Imagine that you are interested in an integrated product suite. Do not just think of one product. Rather think of multiple products under one brand. That applies to making a living online. Do not just engage in one method. Engage in as many as you can. This way, you always have something to fall back on. Also, do not look at online business as a side thing. If you are not ready to make it your main thing, there is a high chance that you will not be able to infuse the amount of effort that is needed.

As a freelancer, remember that there are others in that field. What are you going to do that others are not doing? What touch are you going to add to make your work unique? Websites like the ones which were mentioned (Fiverr, Upwork, etc.) are great places to begin and continue. Procrastination will be your most deadly enemy, look out for it. Each job you undertake adds to your experience. Starting small is the way to go. Most big employers will want you to have an amount of experience you can only have by taking on smaller jobs.

Kindle eBooks is the second way mentioned. Look into them. Check out EpicRights for research material. Get people to write for you and test and expand your skills as a marketer. Get people to design your covers and talk to people who have experience using Kindle eBooks.

Affiliate Marketing is a very passive method of generating income. Remember; pick your products based on your audience. You can pick as many as your ability can take. Find products that you use, you believe in and you trust, and recommend them to your audience or other people.

Advertising is an equally passive method. It is similar but should not be confused with affiliate marketing. Visit Socialbluebook to know exactly how much you are worth and how much you should charge to the barest minimum. Create content and advertise it.

The fifth way is through online courses. While you are doing the advertising, learning all those methods, and looking for trends, take the time to ask your audience what they want in a course. What do they want to see in a course? What can interest them? What do they need? What do they want to know about? Get knowledge on it, and make an online course. Give them the knowledge they want, so they don't have to pass through the stress you did to acquire it. Go through teachable and other recommended sites.

Investing in stocks is the next method. Remember to disregard any stock advice given by anyone who is not a professional. Talk is cheap, and in the end, it will be your money to go for it. Watch the news for the latest information on stocks. Do business with a brokerage firm of good repute. Hearing from one source is not enough. One excellent decision can make a huge difference, and similarly, a terrible decision can do the same.

The last way mentioned is through royalties. Similar to freelancing, your skills gain you money. If you have any skills that are specified and crafty go ahead and look into how you can get royalties from your art.

People around the world are making incomes of up to six figures through passive income generating. They exploit these seven avenues and more. Nothing stops you from attaining the level of success which they have.

One thing to remember is that although these methods are passive, it does not mean that they will require little input from you. Other people are trying to earn money using these same methods. The little extra you add will go a long way.

In case you do not have YouTube account, it would be smart move to get one. From there, getting a channel is as close as you can ever imagine it.

Remember: The higher the barrier, the lesser the population.

www.ingramcontent.com/pod-product-compliance
Lightning Source LLC
Chambersburg PA
CBHW030519220526
45464CB00006B/2872